Preface

MathExpress - Speed Math Strategies series aims at developing new ways in acquiring mathematics skills for effective and enjoyable learning. It helps pupils improve speed and accuracy through the simple, fun-to-learn strategies introduced at different levels.

- ➲ Level 1 - Addition & Subtraction Within 100
- ➲ Level 2 - Addition & Subtraction Within 1000
- ➲ Level 3 - More On Addition & Subtraction / Multiplication & Division
- ➲ Level 4 - More On Multiplication / Decimals
- ➲ Level 5 - Fractions / Checking Answers
- ➲ Level 6 - Percentage / Other Topics

This series of books is recommended for both High and Low Achievers.

High Achievers - Challenging themselves to master speedy mental calculations, developing the ability to analyse, simplify and think laterally.

Low Achievers - Developing an interest for working, playing and experimenting with numbers as well as increasing their self-esteem. No more 'maths-phobia'!

The faster and easier method we use, the fewer mistakes we make!

Li Fanglan

This book belongs to:

Vidya

Contents

Express Strategy 1

Can you get the answers in 10 seconds?

(a)   4 + 11 = ?

(b)   15 + 3 = ?

Your Answer: (a) _15 18_

(b) _18_

Time Taken: _____ seconds

What is the value of <u>4 + 11</u>?

Solution:

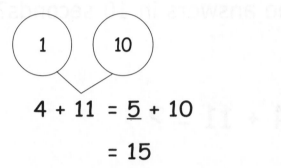

4 + 11 = <u>5</u> + 10

= 15

1 and 10 make 11.

Add 4 and 1 before adding 10.

Addition - Regroup Into Tens And Ones

What is the value of <u>15 + 3</u>?

Solution:

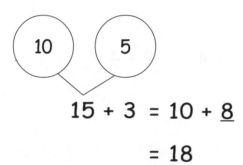

$$15 + 3 = 10 + \underline{8}$$
$$= 18$$

10 and 5 make 15.

Add 5 and 3 before adding 10.

Addition - Regroup Into Tens And Ones

Do the sums using the strategy.

1. 2 + 11   2. 11 + 3

3. 3 + 12   4. 12 + 4

5. 4 + 13   6. 13 + 5

7. 7 + 12   8. 14 + 5

9. 5 + 14   10. 16 + 3

Solve the problems using the strategy.

1.   12 boys are playing at a playground.
3 girls join them.
How many children are at the playground altogether?

2.   Andy has 6 big balls and 13 small balls.
How many balls does he have altogether?

Date: _____   Time Taken: _____   Marks:___/10

Do the following mentally. Write your answers in the boxes provided.

1.   3 + 11 =

2.   11 + 4 =

3.   5 + 12 =

4.   12 + 6 =

5.   4 + 15 =

6.   16 + 2 =

7.   7 + 11 =

8.   11 + 8 =

9.   Sam has 15 storybooks.
      His sister has 3 storybooks.
      How many storybooks do they have altogether?

Express Strategy 2

Can you get the answers in 10 seconds?

(a) $5 + 6 = ?$

(b) $6 + 7 = ?$

Your Answer: (a) _____

(b) _____

Time Taken: _____ seconds

What is the value of <u>5 + 6</u>?

Solution:

5   + 1

5 + 6 = <u>10</u> + 1

        = 11

5 and 5 make 10.

Rewrite 6 as 5 + 1.

Add 5 and 5 to get 10 before adding 1.

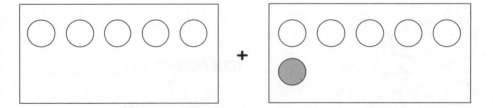

Addition - Use Number Bonds To Make 10 (1)

What is the value of <u>6 + 7</u>?

Solution:

$$\overset{\overset{\displaystyle 5 \quad +1}{\diagdown\!\diagup}}{6} \quad + \quad \overset{\overset{\displaystyle 5 \quad +2}{\diagdown\!\diagup}}{7} \quad = \quad \underline{10} \;+\; \underline{3}$$

$$= 13$$

5 and 5 make 10.

Rewrite 6 as 5 + 1 and 7 as 5 + 2.

Add 5 and 5 to get 10 before adding 1 and 2.

Addition - Use Number Bonds To Make 10 (1)

Do the sums using the strategy.

1.   5 + 7

2.   5 + 8

3.   5 + 9

4.   6 + 5

5.   7 + 5

6.   8 + 5

7.   9 + 5

8.   6 + 6

9.   9 + 6

10.   7 + 7

Solve the problems using the strategy.

1. Jimmy has 5 toy cars.
   Alan has 8 toy cars.
   How many toy cars do they have altogether?

2. Jessie has 6 balloons.
   Mummy gives her another 8 balloons.
   How many balloons does Jessie have now?

Date: _____   Time Taken: _____   Marks:___/10

Do the following mentally. Write your answers in the boxes provided.

1.   5 + 6 = [   ]   2.   5 + 8 = [   ]

3.   9 + 5 = [   ]   4.   7 + 5 = [   ]

5.   7 + 6 = [   ]   6.   7 + 7 = [   ]

7.   6 + 9 = [   ]   8.   8 + 8 = [   ]

9.   There are 9 mangoes in a basket.
      Joyce puts in another 5 mangoes.
      How many mangoes are there in the basket now?

[   ]

Express Strategy 3

Can you get the answers in 10 seconds?

(a)   9 + 3 = ?

(b)   7 + 8 = ?

Your Answer: (a) _____

(b) _____

Time Taken: _____ seconds

What is the value of <u>9 + 3</u>?

Solution:

$$9 + 3 = \underline{10} + 2$$
$$= 12$$

9 and 1 make 10.

Rewrite 3 as 1 + 2.

Add 1 to 9 to get 10 before adding 2.

Addition - Use Number Bonds To Make 10 (2)

What is the value of 7 + 8?

Solution:

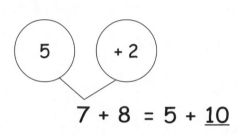

7 + 8 = 5 + <u>10</u>

= 15

2 and 8 make 10.

Rewrite 7 as 5 + 2.

Add 2 to 8 to get 10 before adding 5.

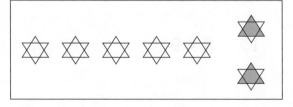 +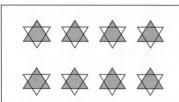

Addition - Use Number Bonds To Make 10 (2)

Worksheet 3A

Do the sums using the strategy.

1.   9 + 2

2.   9 + 4

3.   9 + 5

4.   9 + 6

5.   8 + 3

6.   8 + 5

7.   6 + 9

8.   7 + 9

9.   8 + 8

10.   8 + 9

Solve the problems using the strategy.

1.   Mary has 8 flowers.
     Minah has 4 more flowers than Mary.
     How many flowers does Minah have?

2.   Nick has 6 toy cars.
     He has 8 more toy boats than toy cars.
     How many toy boats does he have?

Date: _____   Time Taken: _____   Marks: ___/10

Do the following mentally. Write your answers in the boxes provided.

1.   2 + 9 = ☐   2.   9 + 5 = ☐

3.   8 + 3 = ☐   4.   4 + 8 = ☐

5.   7 + 7 = ☐   6.   6 + 6 = ☐

7.   8 + 8 = ☐   8.   9 + 9 = ☐

9.   A number is 4 more than 9.
      What is the number?

☐

Express Strategy 4

Can you get the answers in 10 seconds?

(a)   7 - 4 = ?

(b)   9 - 5 = ?

Your Answer: (a) _____

(b) _____

Time Taken: _____ seconds

What is the value of <u>7 - 4</u>?

Solution:

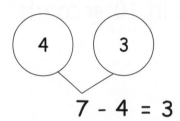

7 - 4 = 3

4 and 3 make 7.

Subtract 4 from 4, leaving 3 as the answer.

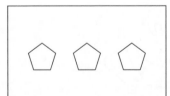

Subtraction - Use Number Bonds

What is the value of <u>9 - 5</u>?

Solution:

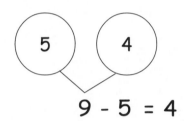

9 - 5 = 4

5 and 4 make 9.

Subtract 5 from 5, leaving 4 as the answer.

Subtraction - Use Number Bonds

Do the sums using the strategy.

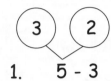

1.   5 - 3

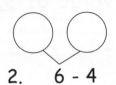

2.   6 - 4

3.   8 - 3

4.   8 - 5

5.   9 - 2

6.   7 - 5

7.   9 - 4

8.   8 - 6

9.   9 - 3

10.   9 - 7

Solve the problems using the strategy.

1. There are 8 children in a group.
    3 of them are boys.
    How many girls are there?

2. Nora and Fatimah have 9 comic books altogether.
    Nora has 6 comic books.
    How many comic books does Fatimah have?

Speed & Accuracy Test 4

Date: _____   Time Taken: _____   Marks:___/10

Do the following mentally. Write your answers in the boxes provided.

1.   6 - 2 =

2.   7 - 2 =

3.   6 - 5 =

4.   8 - 4 =

5.   7 - 3 =

6.   6 - 3 =

7.   9 - 4 =

8.   9 - 6 =

9.   Peter has 7 balloons.
      4 balloons burst.
      How many balloons are left?

Express Strategy 5

Can you get the answers in 10 seconds?

(a)   16 - 5 = ?

(b)   18 - 3 = ?

Your Answer: (a) _____

(b) _____

Time Taken: _____ seconds

What is the value of <u>16 - 5</u>?

Solution:

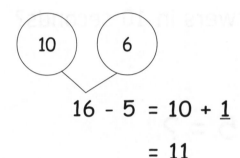

$$16 - 5 = 10 + \underline{1}$$
$$= 11$$

10 and 6 make 16.

Subtract 5 from 6 before adding 10.

Subtraction - Regroup Into Tens And Ones (1)

What is the value of <u>18 - 3</u>?

Solution:

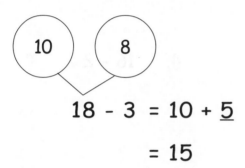

18 - 3 = 10 + <u>5</u>

= 15

10 and 8 make 18.

Subtract 3 from 8 before adding 10.

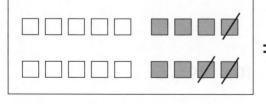 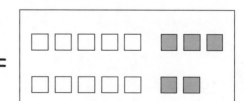

Subtraction - Regroup Into Tens And Ones (1)

Do the sums using the strategy.

1.   13 - 2

2.   15 - 1

3.   15 - 3

4.   16 - 2

5.   17 - 5

6.   16 - 4

7.   17 - 3

8.   18 - 5

9.   19 - 7

10.   19 - 5

Solve the problems using the strategy.

1. Elsie has 14 rubber bands.
   She uses 3 rubber bands to tie some books.
   How many rubber bands has she left?

2. There are 19 strawberries in a basket.
   Joe eats some strawberries.
   There are 4 strawberries left.
   How many strawberries does Joe eat?

Speed & Accuracy Test 5

Date: _____   Time Taken: _____   Marks:___/10

Do the following mentally. Write your answers in the boxes provided.

1.   12 - 1 = ☐

2.   15 - 2 = ☐

3.   16 - 3 = ☐

4.   17 - 4 = ☐

5.   18 - 4 = ☐

6.   17 - 2 = ☐

7.   19 - 3 = ☐

8.   19 - 4 = ☐

9.   Gigi has 19 sweets.
     She gives 6 sweets to her brother.
     How many sweets has she left?

☐

Express Strategy 6

Can you get the answers in 10 seconds?

(a)   12 - 9 = ?

(b)   14 - 8 = ?

Your Answer: (a) _____

(b) _____

Time Taken: _____ seconds

What is the value of <u>12 - 9</u>?

Solution:

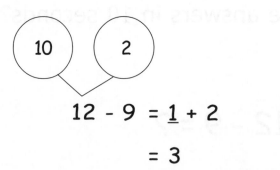

12 - 9 = <u>1</u> + 2

= 3

10 and 2 make 12.

Subtract 9 from 10 before adding 2.

Subtraction - Regroup Into Tens And Ones (2)

What is the value of <u>14 - 8</u>?

Solution:

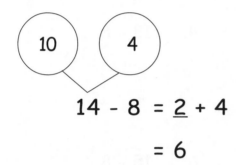

14 - 8 = <u>2</u> + 4

   = 6

10 and 4 make 14.

Subtract 8 from 10 before adding 4.

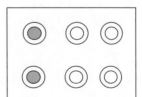

Subtraction - Regroup Into Tens And Ones (2)

Do the sums using the strategy.

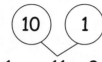

1.   11 - 9

2.   13 - 9

3.   12 - 8

4.   13 - 8

5.   14 - 9

6.   15 - 8

7.   16 - 9

8.   17 - 8

9.   16 - 7

10.   13 - 6

Solve the problems using the strategy.

1.   A number is 9 less than 15.
      What is the number?

2.   There are 14 balls in a box.
      6 balls are brown.
      The rest are blue.
      How many blue balls are there?

Speed & Accuracy Test 6

Date: _____   Time Taken: _____   Marks:___/10

Do the following mentally. Write your answers in the boxes provided.

1. 13 - 9 =

2. 11 - 8 =

3. 17 - 9 =

4. 12 - 7 =

5. 15 - 7 =

6. 16 - 8 =

7. 11 - 3 =

8. 15 - 6 =

9. There are 12 eggs on a plate.
    5 eggs are broken.
    How many eggs are not broken?

Express Strategy 7

Can you get the answers in 10 seconds?

(a) 7 + 4 + 3 = ?

(b) 4 + 8 + 2 = ?

Your Answer: (a) _____

(b) _____

Time Taken: _____ seconds

What is the value of <u>7 + 4 + 3</u>?

Solution:

$$7 + 4 + 3 = \underline{10} + 4$$
$$= 14$$

7 and 3 make 10.

Add 7 and 3 before adding 4.

 + 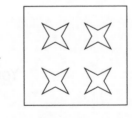 +

Addition - Pair Them Up

What is the value of <u>4 + 8 + 2</u>?

Solution:

$$4 + 8 + 2 = 4 + \underline{10}$$
$$= 14$$

8 and 2 make 10.

Add 8 and 2 before adding 4.

Addition - Pair Them Up

Do the sums using the strategy.

1.   9 + 4 + 1

2.   8 + 3 + 2

3.   3 + 6 + 7

4.   4 + 5 + 6

5.   5 + 8 + 5

6.   6 + 9 + 1

7.   3 + 2 + 8

8.   8 + 7 + 3

9.   9 + 4 + 6

10. 7 + 5 + 5

Solve the problems using the strategy.

1. Ms Ee has 4 red pens, 3 blue pens and 6 black pens.
    How many pens does she have altogether?

2. 5 boys and 7 girls are jogging.
    3 teachers join them.
    How many people are jogging now?

Date: _____   Time Taken: _____   Marks:____/10

Do the following mentally. Write your answers in the boxes provided.

1.   5 + 4 + 5 =

2.   2 + 5 + 8 =

3.   2 + 7 + 3 =

4.   3 + 6 + 4 =

5.   5 + 9 + 1 =

6.   6 + 2 + 8 =

7.   7 + 9 + 3 =

8.   8 + 6 + 4 =

9.   Ben has 4 red marbles, 7 blue marbles and 6 black marbles. How many marbles does he have altogether?

Express Strategy 8

Can you get the answers in 10 seconds?

(a) 4 + 2 - 3 = ?

(b) 3 + 6 - 5 = ?

Your Answer: (a) _____

(b) _____

Time Taken: _____ seconds

What is the value of <u>4 + 2 - 3</u>?

Solution:

$$4 + 2 - 3 = \underline{1} + 2$$
$$= 3$$

Subtract 3 from 4 before adding 2.

Addition & Subtraction - Who Goes First

What is the value of 3 + 6 - 5?

Solution:

3 + 6 - 5 = 3 + <u>1</u>

             = 4

Subtract 5 from 6 before adding 3.

Addition & Subtraction - Who Goes First

Do the sums using the strategy.

1. $\overparen{5 + 3} - 4$

2. $\overparen{6 + 4} - 5$

3. $3 + 1 - 2$

4. $5 + 2 - 4$

5. $7 + 2 - 5$

6. $4 + 7 - 6$

7. $3 + 9 - 8$

8. $5 + 8 - 6$

9. $4 + 9 - 6$

10. $3 + 9 - 5$

Solve the problems using the strategy.

1. Eileen has 5 red flowers and 1 white flower.
    She gives 4 flowers to her best friend.
    How many flowers has she left?

2. There are 5 butter cookies and 9 peanut cookies on a plate.
    Olive eats 7 cookies.
    How many cookies are left?

Speed & Accuracy Test 8

Date: _____   Time Taken: _____   Marks: ___/10

Do the following mentally. Write your answers in the boxes provided.

1.   3 + 6 - 4 =

2.   4 + 8 - 6 =

3.   8 + 5 - 7 =

4.   5 + 2 - 3 =

5.   7 + 4 - 5 =

6.   3 + 8 - 6 =

7.   9 + 6 - 7 =

8.   5 + 9 - 6 =

9.   Rama has 4 peanut cookies and 7 chocolate cookies.
     She gives 5 cookies to her brother.
     How many cookies has she left?

Express Strategy 9

Can you get the answers in 10 seconds?

(a)   4 + 3 - 5 = ?

(b)   5 + 7 - 9 = ?

Your Answer: (a) _____

(b) _____

Time Taken: _____ seconds

What is the value of <u>4 + 3 - 5</u>?

Solution:

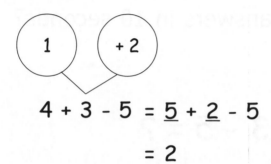

4 + 3 - 5 = <u>5</u> + <u>2</u> - 5

= 2

4 is 1 less than 5.

Rewrite 3 as 1 + 2. Add 1 to 4 to get 5.

Subtract 5 from 5, leaving 2 as the answer.

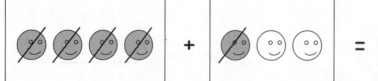

Addition & Subtraction - Tapping On Others

What is the value of 5 + 7 - 9?

Solution:

3   + 2

5 + 7 - 9 = 3 + 9 - 9

= 3

7 is 2 less than 9.

Rewrite 5 as 3 + 2. Add 2 to 7 to get 9.

Subtract 9 from 9, leaving 3 as the answer.

Addition & Subtraction - Tapping On Others

Do the sums using the strategy.

1. 3 + 2 - 4

2. 5 + 4 - 6

3. 6 + 4 - 7

4. 7 + 4 - 9

5. 6 + 5 - 8

6. 4 + 7 - 8

7. 3 + 8 - 9

8. 4 + 5 - 7

9. 6 + 7 - 9

10. 7 + 7 - 9

Solve the problems using the strategy.

1.   There are 3 fruit tarts and 5 egg tarts on a plate.
     Ali eats 6 tarts.
     How many tarts are left?

2.   Ann has 4 Singapore stamps and 8 Malaysia stamps.
     She gives 9 stamps to her best friend.
     How many stamps has Ann left?

Speed & Accuracy Test 9

Date: _____   Time Taken: _____   Marks:___/10

Do the following mentally. Write your answers in the boxes provided.

1.   3 + 5 - 6 =

2.   5 + 6 - 7 =

3.   4 + 6 - 8 =

4.   7 + 5 - 8 =

5.   4 + 7 - 9 =

6.   6 + 7 - 8 =

7.   8 + 8 - 9 =

8.   7 + 3 - 9 =

9.   Mrs Kumar bakes 4 chocolate cakes and 8 fruit cakes.
     She sells 9 cakes.
     How many cakes are left?

Express Strategy 10

Can you get the answers in 10 seconds?

(a) 11 - 2 + 3 = ?

(b) 12 - 5 + 4 = ?

Your Answer: (a) _____

(b) _____

Time Taken: _____ seconds

What is the value of <u>11 - 2 + 3</u>?

Solution:

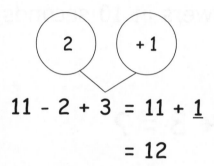

11 - 2 + 3 = 11 + <u>1</u>

= 12

3 is 1 more than 2.

Rewrite 3 as 2 + 1.

Subtract 2 from 2 before adding 11 and 1.

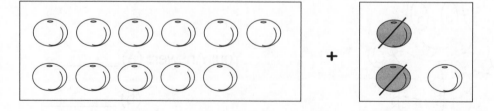

Addition & Subtraction - Mixed Strategies

What is the value of <u>12 - 5 + 4</u>?

Solution:

(11) (+ 1)

12 - 5 + 4 = 11 - 5 + <u>5</u>

= 11

4 is 1 less than 5.

Rewrite 12 as 11 + 1. Add 1 to 4 to get 5.

Subtract 5 from 5 before adding 11.

 **+**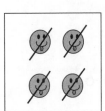

Addition & Subtraction - Mixed Strategies

Worksheet 10A

Do the sums using the strategy.

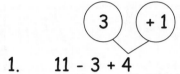

1.   11 - 3 + 4

2.   11 - 5 + 6

3.   12 - 4 + 5

4.   13 - 5 + 6

5.   14 - 5 + 7

6.   12 - 4 + 3

7.   12 - 7 + 6

8.   13 - 6 + 5

9.   15 - 8 + 6

10. 17 - 9 + 6

Worksheet 10B

Solve the problems using the strategy.

1. David has 12 toy cars.
   He gives 5 toy cars to his brother.
   His father buys him another 6 toy cars.
   How many toy cars does David have now?

2. June has 14 goldfish.
   She gives 7 goldfish to her sister.
   Her mother buys her another 5 goldfish.
   How many goldfish does June have now?

Date: _____   Time Taken: _____   Marks: ___/10

Do the following mentally. Write your answers in the boxes provided.

1.   12 - 3 + 4 = ☐   2.   13 - 4 + 5 = ☐

3.   12 - 4 + 6 = ☐   4.   15 - 7 + 9 = ☐

5.   12 - 6 + 5 = ☐   6.   13 - 5 + 4 = ☐

7.   16 - 8 + 6 = ☐   8.   15 - 9 + 6 = ☐

9.   Arif has 15 storybooks.
     He gives 8 storybooks to his friend.
     His mother buys him another 7 storybooks.
     How many storybooks does he have now?

☐

Express Strategy 11

Can you get the answers in 10 seconds?

(a)   29 + 6 = ?

(b)   13 + 18 = ?

Your Answer: (a) _____

(b) _____

Time Taken: _____ seconds

What is the value of <u>29 + 6</u>?

Solution:

$$\overset{\overset{\textstyle 1 \quad +5}{}}{29 + 6} = \underline{30} + \underline{5}$$
$$= 35$$

29 and 1 make 30.

Rewrite 6 as 1 + 5.

Add 1 to 29 to get 30 before adding 5.

Addition - Make Tens

What is the value of <u>13 + 18</u>?

Solution:

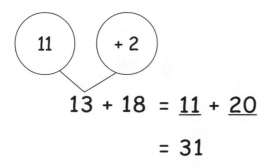

$$13 + 18 = \underline{11} + \underline{20}$$
$$= 31$$

18 and 2 make 20.

Rewrite 13 as 11 + 2.

Add 2 to 18 to get 20 before adding 11.

Addition - Make Tens

Worksheet 11A

Do the sums using the strategy.

1. 19 + 5

2. 29 + 7

3. 18 + 6

4. 8 + 28

5. 5 + 27

6. 13 + 19

7. 16 + 19

8. 15 + 18

9. 17 + 17

10. 16 + 16

Solve the problems using the strategy.

1. Raj has 29 toy soldiers.
   Leo has 5 more toy soldiers than Raj.
   How many toy soldiers does Leo have?

2. Victor makes 17 paper cranes.
   His sister makes 18 paper cranes.
   How many paper cranes do they make altogether?

Speed & Accuracy Test 11

Date: _____   Time Taken: _____   Marks:___/10

Do the following mentally. Write your answers in the boxes provided.

1.   7 + 19 =

2.   8 + 29 =

3.   18 + 9 =

4.   17 + 6 =

5.   14 + 19 =

6.   19 + 15 =

7.   18 + 16 =

8.   19 + 18 =

9.   Frank has 28 toy cars.
      Sam has 7 more toy cars than Frank.
      How many toy cars does Sam have?

Express Strategy 12

Can you get the answers in 10 seconds?

(a)   27 - 9 = ?

(b)   35 - 18 = ?

Your Answer: (a) _____

(b) _____

Time Taken: _____ seconds

What is the value of <u>27 - 9</u>?

Solution:

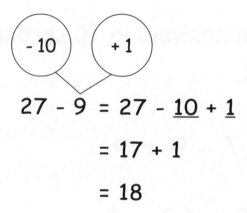

$$27 - 9 = 27 - \underline{10} + \underline{1}$$
$$= 17 + 1$$
$$= 18$$

9 is 1 less than 10.

Subtract 10 from 27 before adding 1.

Subtraction - Use Tens

What is the value of <u>35 - 18</u>?

Solution:

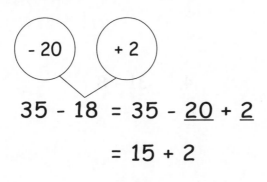

$$35 - 18 = 35 - \underline{20} + \underline{2}$$
$$= 15 + 2$$
$$= 17$$

18 is 2 less than 20.

Subtract 20 from 35 before adding 2.

Subtraction - Use Tens

Do the sums using the strategy.

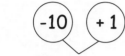

1. 21 - 9

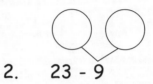

2. 23 - 9

3. 25 - 8

4. 31 - 8

5. 32 - 19

6. 35 - 29

7. 25 - 18

8. 27 - 18

9. 31 - 28

10. 36 - 27

Solve the problems using the strategy.

1. Dolly and Joyce have 26 phone cards altogether.
   Dolly has 19 phone cards.
   How many phone cards does Joyce have?

2. Bryan has 31 sweets.
   He gives some sweets to his brother.
   He has 18 sweets left after that.
   How many sweets does Bryan give to his brother?

Date: _____   Time Taken: _____   Marks:___/10

Do the following mentally. Write your answers in the boxes provided.

1.   24 - 9 =

2.   22 - 8 =

3.   31 - 9 =

4.   32 - 8 =

5.   33 - 19 =

6.   26 - 18 =

7.   35 - 19 =

8.   37 - 28 =

9.   Emily prepares 36 balloons for a party.
      18 balloons are red and the rest are yellow.
      How many yellow balloons are there?

Express Strategy 13

Can you get the answers in 10 seconds?

(a)   26 + 49 = ?

(b)   58 + 37 = ?

Your Answer: (a) _____

(b) _____

Time Taken: _____ seconds

What is the value of <u>26 + 49</u>?

Solution:

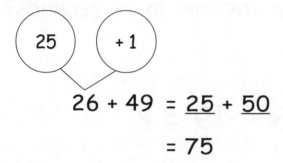

$$26 + 49 = \underline{25} + \underline{50}$$

$$= 75$$

> 1 and 49 make 50.
>
> Rewrite 26 as 25 + 1.
>
> Add 1 to 49 to get 50 before adding 25.

Addition - Make Tens

What is the value of <u>58 + 37</u>?

Solution:

$$58 + 37 = \underline{60} + \underline{35}$$

$$= 95$$

> 58 and 2 make 60.
>
> Rewrite 37 as 2 + 35.
>
> Add 2 to 58 to get 60 before adding 35.

Addition - Make Tens

Worksheet 13A

Do the sums using the strategy.

1. 23 + 39

2. 17 + 29

3. 38 + 19

4. 25 + 59

5. 29 + 43

6. 49 + 37

7. 16 + 38

8. 28 + 35

9. 47 + 48

10. 57 + 24

Solve the problems using the strategy.

1. Jimmy has $23.
   His brother has $29.
   How much money do they have altogether?

2. A number is 28 more than 45.
   What is the number?

Date: _____   Time Taken: _____   Marks:____/10

Do the following mentally. Write your answers in the boxes provided.

1.   17 + 29 = ☐

2.   28 + 34 = ☐

3.   39 + 46 = ☐

4.   53 + 19 = ☐

5.   38 + 45 = ☐

6.   68 + 28 = ☐

7.   56 + 39 = ☐

8.   47 + 37 = ☐

9.   Amy folds 38 paper stars.
     Mohan folds 35 paper stars.
     How many paper stars do they fold altogether?

☐

Express Strategy 14

Can you get the answers in 10 seconds?

(a)   81 - 29 = ?

(b)   92 - 38 = ?

Your Answer: (a) 5̶6̶ 5^2

(b) 5̶ 4

Time Taken: a→2 2ᵈ seconds

What is the value of <u>81 - 29</u>?

Solution:

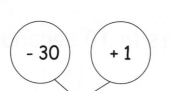

$$81 - 29 = 81 - \underline{30} + \underline{1}$$
$$= 51 + 1$$
$$= 52$$

29 is 1 less than 30.

Subtract 30 from 81 before adding 1.

Subtraction - Use Tens

What is the value of <u>92 - 38</u>?

Solution:

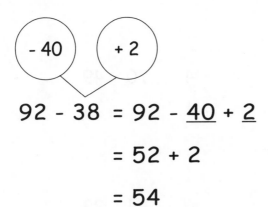

92 - 38 = 92 - <u>40</u> + <u>2</u>

= 52 + 2

= 54

38 is 2 less than 40.

Subtract 40 from 92 before adding 2.

Subtraction - Use Tens

Do the sums using the strategy.

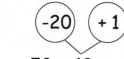

1. 52 - 19

2. 43 - 19

3. 51 - 39

4. 70 - 49

5. 45 - 18

6. 64 - 28

7. 73 - 38

8. 85 - 48

9. 81 - 37

10. 95 - 57

Solve the problems using the strategy.

1. James and his brother have $55.
   James has $29.
   How much money does his brother have?

2. There are 72 pupils in a hall.
   38 of them are girls.
   How many boys are there?

Date: _____   Time Taken: _____   Marks:___/10

Do the following mentally. Write your answers in the boxes provided.

1.   43 - 29 =

2.   51 - 19 =

3.   45 - 38 =

4.   54 - 28 =

5.   70 - 48 =

6.   74 - 37 =

7.   85 - 58 =

8.   93 - 69 =

9.   Irfan has $65.
      He spends $29 to buy a pair of shoes.
      How much money has he left?

$

Date: _____   Time Taken: _____   Marks:___/28

Do the following mentally. Write your answers in the boxes provided.

1. $12 + 3 =$ ☐

2. $8 + 8 =$ ☐

3. $9 + 9 =$ ☐

4. $9 - 6 =$ ☐

5. $19 - 4 =$ ☐

6. $15 - 6 =$ ☐

7. $8 + 6 + 4 =$ ☐

8. $5 + 9 - 6 =$ ☐

9. $7 + 3 - 9 =$ ☐

10. $15 - 9 + 6 =$ ☐

11. $19 + 18 =$ ☐

12. $37 - 28 =$ ☐

13. $47 + 37 =$ ☐

14. $93 - 69 =$ ☐

Date: _____   Time Taken: _____   Marks:___/28

Do the following mentally. Write your answers in the boxes provided.

1.   5 + 13 = ☐

2.   6 + 9 = ☐

3.   8 + 8 = ☐

4.   9 - 4 = ☐

5.   19 - 3 = ☐

6.   11 - 3 = ☐

7.   7 + 9 + 3 = ☐

8.   9 + 6 - 7 = ☐

9.   8 + 8 - 9 = ☐

10.   16 - 8 + 6 = ☐

11.   18 + 16 = ☐

12.   35 - 19 = ☐

13.   56 + 39 = ☐

14.   85 - 58 = ☐

Answer Key And Detailed Solutions

Worksheet 1A

1. 2 + 11
   = 3 + 10
   = 13

2. 11 + 3
   = 10 + 4
   = 14

3. 3 + 12
   = 5 + 10
   = 15

4. 12 + 4
   = 10 + 6
   = 16

5. 4 + 13
   = 7 + 10
   = 17

6. 13 + 5
   = 10 + 8
   = 18

7. 7 + 12
   = 9 + 10
   = 19

8. 14 + 5
   = 10 + 9
   = 19

9. 5 + 14
   = 9 + 10
   = 19

10. 16 + 3
    = 10 + 9
    = 19

Worksheet 1B

1. 12 + 3
   = 10 + 5
   = 15

2. 6 + 13
   = 9 + 10
   = 19

Speed & Accuracy Test 1

1. 3 + 11
   = 4 + 10
   = 14

2. 11 + 4
   = 10 + 5
   = 15

3. 5 + 12
   = 7 + 10
   = 17

4. 12 + 6
   = 10 + 8
   = 18

5. 4 + 15
   = 9 + 10
   = 19

6. 16 + 2
   = 10 + 8
   = 18

7. 7 + 11
   = 8 + 10
   = 18

8. 11 + 8
   = 10 + 9
   = 19

9. 15 + 3
   = 10 + 8
   = 18

Worksheet 2A

1. $5 + 7$
   $= 10 + 2$
   $= 12$

2. $5 + 8$
   $= 10 + 3$
   $= 13$

3. $5 + 9$
   $= 10 + 4$
   $= 14$

4. $6 + 5$
   $= 1 + 10$
   $= 11$

5. $7 + 5$
   $= 2 + 10$
   $= 12$

6. $8 + 5$
   $= 3 + 10$
   $= 13$

7. $9 + 5$
   $= 4 + 10$
   $= 14$

8. $6 + 6$
   $= 10 + 2$
   $= 12$

9. $9 + 6$
   $= 10 + 5$
   $= 15$

10. $7 + 7$
    $= 10 + 4$
    $= 14$

Worksheet 2B

1. $5 + 8$
   $= 10 + 3$
   $= 13$

2. $6 + 8$
   $= 10 + 4$
   $= 14$

Speed & Accuracy Test 2

1. $5 + 6$
   $= 10 + 1$
   $= 11$

2. $5 + 8$
   $= 10 + 3$
   $= 13$

3. $9 + 5$
   $= 4 + 10$
   $= 14$

4. $7 + 5$
   $= 2 + 10$
   $= 12$

5. $7 + 6$
   $= 10 + 3$
   $= 13$

6. $7 + 7$
   $= 10 + 4$
   $= 14$

7. $6 + 9$
   $= 10 + 5$
   $= 15$

8. $8 + 8$
   $= 10 + 6$
   $= 16$

9. $9 + 5$
   $= 4 + 10$
   $= 14$

Worksheet 3A

1. $9 + 2$
$= 10 + 1$
$= 11$

2. $9 + 4$
$= 10 + 3$
$= 13$

3. $9 + 5$
$= 10 + 4$
$= 14$

4. $9 + 6$
$= 10 + 5$
$= 15$

5. $8 + 3$
$= 10 + 1$
$= 11$

6. $8 + 5$
$= 10 + 3$
$= 13$

7. $6 + 9$
$= 5 + 10$
$= 15$

8. $7 + 9$
$= 6 + 10$
$= 16$

9. $8 + 8$
$= 6 + 10$
$= 16$

10. $8 + 9$
$= 7 + 10$
$= 17$

Worksheet 3B

1. $8 + 4$
$= 10 + 2$
$= 12$

2. $6 + 8$
$= 4 + 10$
$= 14$

Speed & Accuracy Test 3

1. $2 + 9$
$= 1 + 10$
$= 11$

2. $9 + 5$
$= 10 + 4$
$= 14$

3. $8 + 3$
$= 10 + 1$
$= 11$

4. $4 + 8$
$= 2 + 10$
$= 12$

5. $7 + 7$
$= 10 + 4$
$= 14$

6. $6 + 6$
$= 10 + 2$
$= 12$

7. $8 + 8$
$= 10 + 6$
$= 16$

8. $9 + 9$
$= 10 + 8$
$= 18$

9. $4 + 9$
$= 3 + 10$
$= 13$

Worksheet 4A

1.   5 - 3
     = 2 + 3 - 3
     = 2

2.   6 - 4
     = 2 + 4 - 4
     = 2

3.   8 - 3
     = 5 + 3 - 3
     = 5

4.   8 - 5
     = 3 + 5 - 5
     = 3

5.   9 - 2
     = 7 + 2 - 2
     = 7

6.   7 - 5
     = 2 + 5 - 5
     = 2

7.   9 - 4
     = 5 + 4 - 4
     = 5

8.   8 - 6
     = 2 + 6 - 6
     = 2

9.   9 - 3
     = 6 + 3 - 3
     = 6

10.   9 - 7
     = 2 + 7 - 7
     = 2

Worksheet 4B

1.   8 - 3
     = 5 + 3 - 3
     = 5

2.   9 - 6
     = 3 + 6 - 6
     = 3

Speed & Accuracy Test 4

1.   6 - 2
     = 4 + 2 - 2
     = 4

2.   7 - 2
     = 5 + 2 - 2
     = 5

3.   6 - 5
     = 1 + 5 - 5
     = 1

4.   8 - 4
     = 4 + 4 - 4
     = 4

5.   7 - 3
     = 4 + 3 - 3
     = 4

6.   6 - 3
     = 3 + 3 - 3
     = 3

7.   9 - 4
     = 5 + 4 - 4
     = 5

8.   9 - 6
     = 3 + 6 - 6
     = 3

9.   7 - 4
     = 3 + 4 - 4
     = 3

Worksheet 5A

1. 13 - 2
    = 10 + 1
    = 11

2. 15 - 1
    = 10 + 4
    = 14

3. 15 - 3
    = 10 + 2
    = 12

4. 16 - 2
    = 10 + 4
    = 14

5. 17 - 5
    = 10 + 2
    = 12

6. 16 - 4
    = 10 + 2
    = 12

7. 17 - 3
    = 10 + 4
    = 14

8. 18 - 5
    = 10 + 3
    = 13

9. 19 - 7
    = 10 + 2
    = 12

10. 19 - 5
    = 10 + 4
    = 14

Worksheet 5B

1. 14 - 3
    = 10 + 1
    = 11

2. 19 - 4
    = 10 + 5
    = 15

Speed & Accuracy Test 5

1. 12 - 1
    = 10 + 1
    = 11

2. 15 - 2
    = 10 + 3
    = 13

3. 16 - 3
    = 10 + 3
    = 13

4. 17 - 4
    = 10 + 3
    = 13

5. 18 - 4
    = 10 + 4
    = 14

6. 17 - 2
    = 10 + 5
    = 15

7. 19 - 3
    = 10 + 6
    = 16

8. 19 - 4
    = 10 + 5
    = 15

9. 19 - 6
    = 10 + 3
    = 13

Worksheet 6A

1. 11 - 9
= 1 + 1
= 2

2. 13 - 9
= 1 + 3
= 4

3. 12 - 8
= 2 + 2
= 4

4. 13 - 8
= 2 + 3
= 5

5. 14 - 9
= 1 + 4
= 5

6. 15 - 8
= 2 + 5
= 7

7. 16 - 9
= 1 + 6
= 7

8. 17 - 8
= 2 + 7
= 9

9. 16 - 7
= 3 + 6
= 9

10. 13 - 6
= 4 + 3
= 7

Worksheet 6B

1. 15 - 9
= 1 + 5
= 6

2. 14 - 6
= 4 + 4
= 8

Speed & Accuracy Test 6

1. 13 - 9
= 1 + 3
= 4

2. 11 - 8
= 2 + 1
= 3

3. 17 - 9
= 1 + 7
= 8

4. 12 - 7
= 3 + 2
= 5

5. 15 - 7
= 3 + 5
= 8

6. 16 - 8
= 2 + 6
= 8

7. 11 - 3
= 7 + 1
= 8

8. 15 - 6
= 4 + 5
= 9

9. 12 - 5
= 5 + 2
= 7

Worksheet 7A

1. $9 + 4 + 1$
   $= 10 + 4$
   $= 14$

2. $8 + 3 + 2$
   $= 10 + 3$
   $= 13$

3. $3 + 6 + 7$
   $= 10 + 6$
   $= 16$

4. $4 + 5 + 6$
   $= 10 + 5$
   $= 15$

5. $5 + 8 + 5$
   $= 10 + 8$
   $= 18$

6. $6 + 9 + 1$
   $= 6 + 10$
   $= 16$

7. $3 + 2 + 8$
   $= 3 + 10$
   $= 13$

8. $8 + 7 + 3$
   $= 8 + 10$
   $= 18$

9. $9 + 4 + 6$
   $= 9 + 10$
   $= 19$

10. $7 + 5 + 5$
    $= 7 + 10$
    $= 17$

Worksheet 7B

1. $4 + 3 + 6$
   $= 10 + 3$
   $= 13$

2. $5 + 7 + 3$
   $= 5 + 10$
   $= 15$

Speed & Accuracy Test 7

1. $5 + 4 + 5$
   $= 10 + 4$
   $= 14$

2. $2 + 5 + 8$
   $= 10 + 5$
   $= 15$

3. $2 + 7 + 3$
   $= 2 + 10$
   $= 12$

4. $3 + 6 + 4$
   $= 3 + 10$
   $= 13$

5. $5 + 9 + 1$
   $= 5 + 10$
   $= 15$

6. $6 + 2 + 8$
   $= 6 + 10$
   $= 16$

7. $7 + 9 + 3$
   $= 10 + 9$
   $= 19$

8. $8 + 6 + 4$
   $= 8 + 10$
   $= 18$

9. $4 + 7 + 6$
   $= 10 + 7$
   $= 17$

Worksheet 8A

1. $5 + 3 - 4$
   $= 1 + 3$
   $= 4$

2. $6 + 4 - 5$
   $= 1 + 4$
   $= 5$

3. $3 + 1 - 2$
   $= 1 + 1$
   $= 2$

4. $5 + 2 - 4$
   $= 1 + 2$
   $= 3$

5. $7 + 2 - 5$
   $= 2 + 2$
   $= 4$

6. $4 + 7 - 6$
   $= 4 + 1$
   $= 5$

7. $3 + 9 - 8$
   $= 3 + 1$
   $= 4$

8. $5 + 8 - 6$
   $= 5 + 2$
   $= 7$

9. $4 + 9 - 6$
   $= 4 + 3$
   $= 7$

10. $3 + 9 - 5$
    $= 3 + 4$
    $= 7$

Worksheet 8B

1. $5 + 1 - 4$
   $= 1 + 1$
   $= 2$

2. $5 + 9 - 7$
   $= 5 + 2$
   $= 7$

Speed & Accuracy Test 8

1. $3 + 6 - 4$
   $= 3 + 2$
   $= 5$

2. $4 + 8 - 6$
   $= 4 + 2$
   $= 6$

3. $8 + 5 - 7$
   $= 1 + 5$
   $= 6$

4. $5 + 2 - 3$
   $= 2 + 2$
   $= 4$

5. $7 + 4 - 5$
   $= 2 + 4$
   $= 6$

6. $3 + 8 - 6$
   $= 3 + 2$
   $= 5$

7. $9 + 6 - 7$
   $= 2 + 6$
   $= 8$

8. $5 + 9 - 6$
   $= 5 + 3$
   $= 8$

9. $4 + 7 - 5$
   $= 4 + 2$
   $= 6$

Worksheet 9A

1. 3 + 2 - 4
    = 4 + 1 - 4
    = 1

2. 5 + 4 - 6
    = 6 + 3 - 6
    = 3

3. 6 + 4 - 7
    = 7 + 3 - 7
    = 3

4. 7 + 4 - 9
    = 9 + 2 - 9
    = 2

5. 6 + 5 - 8
    = 8 + 3 - 8
    = 3

6. 4 + 7 - 8
    = 3 + 8 - 8
    = 3

7. 3 + 8 - 9
    = 2 + 9 - 9
    = 2

8. 4 + 5 - 7
    = 2 + 7 - 7
    = 2

9. 6 + 7 - 9
    = 4 + 9 - 9
    = 4

10. 7 + 7 - 9
    = 5 + 9 - 9
    = 5

Worksheet 9B

1. 3 + 5 - 6
    = 2 + 6 - 6
    = 2

2. 4 + 8 - 9
    = 3 + 9 - 9
    = 3

Speed & Accuracy Test 9

1. 3 + 5 - 6
    = 2 + 6 - 6
    = 2

2. 5 + 6 - 7
    = 4 + 7 - 7
    = 4

3. 4 + 6 - 8
    = 2 + 8 - 8
    = 2

4. 7 + 5 - 8
    = 8 + 4 - 8
    = 4

5. 4 + 7 - 9
    = 2 + 9 - 9
    = 2

6. 6 + 7 - 8
    = 5 + 8 - 8
    = 5

7. 8 + 8 - 9
    = 7 + 9 - 9
    = 7

8. 7 + 3 - 9
    = 9 + 1 - 9
    = 1

9. 4 + 8 - 9
    = 3 + 9 - 9
    = 3

Worksheet 10A

1. 11 - 3 + 4
   = 11 + 1
   = 12

2. 11 - 5 + 6
   = 11 + 1
   = 12

3. 12 - 4 + 5
   = 12 + 1
   = 13

4. 13 - 5 + 6
   = 13 + 1
   = 14

5. 14 - 5 + 7
   = 14 + 2
   = 16

6. 12 - 4 + 3
   = 11 - 4 + 4
   = 11

7. 12 - 7 + 6
   = 11 - 7 + 7
   = 11

8. 13 - 6 + 5
   = 12 - 6 + 6
   = 12

9. 15 - 8 + 6
   = 13 - 8 + 8
   = 13

10. 17 - 9 + 6
    = 14 - 9 + 9
    = 14

Worksheet 10B

1. 12 - 5 + 6
   = 12 + 1
   = 13

2. 14 - 7 + 5
   = 12 - 7 + 7
   = 12

Speed & Accuracy Test 10

1. 12 - 3 + 4
   = 12 + 1
   = 13

2. 13 - 4 + 5
   = 13 + 1
   = 14

3. 12 - 4 + 6
   = 12 + 2
   = 14

4. 15 - 7 + 9
   = 15 + 2
   = 17

5. 12 - 6 + 5
   = 11 - 6 + 6
   = 11

6. 13 - 5 + 4
   = 12 - 5 + 5
   = 12

7. 16 - 8 + 6
   = 14 - 8 + 8
   = 14

8. 15 - 9 + 6
   = 12 - 9 + 9
   = 12

9. 15 - 8 + 7
   = 14 - 8 + 8
   = 14

Worksheet 11A

1. 19 + 5
    = 20 + 4
    = 24

2. 29 + 7
    = 30 + 6
    = 36

3. 18 + 6
    = 20 + 4
    = 24

4. 8 + 28
    = 6 + 30
    = 36

5. 5 + 27
    = 2 + 30
    = 32

6. 13 + 19
    = 12 + 20
    = 32

7. 16 + 19
    = 15 + 20
    = 35

8. 15 + 18
    = 13 + 20
    = 33

9. 17 + 17
    = 14 + 20
    = 34

10. 16 + 16
    = 12 + 20
    = 32

Worksheet 11B

1. 29 + 5
    = 30 + 4
    = 34

2. 17 + 18
    = 15 + 20
    = 35

Speed & Accuracy Test 11

1. 7 + 19
    = 6 + 20
    = 26

2. 8 + 29
    = 7 + 30
    = 37

3. 18 + 9
    = 20 + 7
    = 27

4. 17 + 6
    = 20 + 3
    = 23

5. 14 + 19
    = 13 + 20
    = 33

6. 19 + 15
    = 20 + 14
    = 34

7. 18 + 16
    = 20 + 14
    = 34

8. 19 + 18
    = 20 + 17
    = 37

9. 28 + 7
    = 30 + 5
    = 35

Worksheet 12A

1. $21 - 9$
   $= 21 - 10 + 1$
   $= 12$

2. $23 - 9$
   $= 23 - 10 + 1$
   $= 14$

3. $25 - 8$
   $= 25 - 10 + 2$
   $= 17$

4. $31 - 8$
   $= 31 - 10 + 2$
   $= 23$

5. $32 - 19$
   $= 32 - 20 + 1$
   $= 13$

6. $35 - 29$
   $= 35 - 30 + 1$
   $= 6$

7. $25 - 18$
   $= 25 - 20 + 2$
   $= 7$

8. $27 - 18$
   $= 27 - 20 + 2$
   $= 9$

9. $31 - 28$
   $= 31 - 30 + 2$
   $= 3$

10. $36 - 27$
    $= 36 - 30 + 3$
    $= 9$

Worksheet 12B

1. $26 - 19$
   $= 26 - 20 + 1$
   $= 7$

2. $31 - 18$
   $= 31 - 20 + 2$
   $= 13$

Speed & Accuracy Test 12

1. $24 - 9$
   $= 24 - 10 + 1$
   $= 15$

2. $22 - 8$
   $= 22 - 10 + 2$
   $= 14$

3. $31 - 9$
   $= 31 - 10 + 1$
   $= 22$

4. $32 - 8$
   $= 32 - 10 + 2$
   $= 24$

5. $33 - 19$
   $= 33 - 20 + 1$
   $= 14$

6. $26 - 18$
   $= 26 - 20 + 2$
   $= 8$

7. $35 - 19$
   $= 35 - 20 + 1$
   $= 16$

8. $37 - 28$
   $= 37 - 30 + 2$
   $= 9$

9. $36 - 18$
   $= 36 - 20 + 2$
   $= 18$

Worksheet 13A

1. 23 + 39
= 22 + 40
= 62

2. 17 + 29
= 16 + 30
= 46

3. 38 + 19
= 37 + 20
= 57

4. 25 + 59
= 24 + 60
= 84

5. 29 + 43
= 30 + 42
= 72

6. 49 + 37
= 50 + 36
= 86

7. 16 + 38
= 14 + 40
= 54

8. 28 + 35
= 30 + 33
= 63

9. 47 + 48
= 45 + 50
= 95

10. 57 + 24
= 60 + 21
= 81

Worksheet 13B

1. 29 + 23
= 30 + 22
= $52

2. 45 + 28
= 43 + 30
= 73

Speed & Accuracy Test 13

1. 17 + 29
= 16 + 30
= 46

2. 28 + 34
= 30 + 32
= 62

3. 39 + 46
= 40 + 45
= 85

4. 53 + 19
= 52 + 20
= 72

5. 38 + 45
= 40 + 43
= 83

6. 68 + 28
= 70 + 26
= 96

7. 56 + 39
= 55 + 40
= 95

8. 47 + 37
= 50 + 34
= 84

9. 38 + 35
= 40 + 33
= 73

Worksheet 14A

1. 52 - 19
   = 52 - 20 + 1
   = 33

2. 43 - 19
   = 43 - 20 + 1
   = 24

3. 51 - 39
   = 51 - 40 + 1
   = 12

4. 70 - 49
   = 70 - 50 + 1
   = 21

5. 45 - 18
   = 45 - 20 + 2
   = 27

6. 64 - 28
   = 64 - 30 + 2
   = 36

7. 73 - 38
   = 73 - 40 + 2
   = 35

8. 85 - 48
   = 85 - 50 + 2
   = 37

9. 81 - 37
   = 81 - 40 + 3
   = 44

10. 95 - 57
    = 95 - 60 + 3
    = 38

Worksheet 14B

1. 55 - 29
   = 55 - 30 + 1
   = $26

2. 72 - 38
   = 72 - 40 + 2
   = 34

Speed & Accuracy Test 14

1. 43 - 29
   = 43 - 30 + 1
   = 14

2. 51 - 19
   = 51 - 20 + 1
   = 32

3. 45 - 38
   = 45 - 40 + 2
   = 7

4. 54 - 28
   = 54 - 30 + 2
   = 26

5. 70 - 48
   = 70 - 50 + 2
   = 22

6. 74 - 37
   = 74 - 40 + 3
   = 37

7. 85 - 58
   = 85 - 60 + 2
   = 27

8. 93 - 69
   = 93 - 70 + 1
   = 24

9. 65 - 29
   = 65 - 30 + 1
   = $36

Diagnostic Test 1

1. $12 + 3 = 10 + 5 = 15$

2. $8 + 8 = 10 + 6 = 16$

3. $9 + 9 = 10 + 8 = 18$

4. $9 - 6 = 3 + 6 - 6 = 3$

5. $19 - 4 = 10 + 5 = 15$

6. $15 - 6 = 4 + 5 = 9$

7. $8 + 6 + 4 = 8 + 10 = 18$

8. $5 + 9 - 6 = 5 + 3 = 8$

9. $7 + 3 - 9 = 9 + 1 - 9 = 1$

10. $15 - 9 + 6 = 12 - 9 + 9 = 12$

11. $19 + 18 = 20 + 17 = 37$

12. $37 - 28 = 37 - 30 + 2 = 9$

13. $47 + 37 = 50 + 34 = 84$

14. $93 - 69 = 93 - 70 + 1 = 24$

Diagnostic Test 2

1. $5 + 13 = 8 + 10 = 18$

2. $6 + 9 = 10 + 5 = 15$

3. $8 + 8 = 10 + 6 = 16$

4. $9 - 4 = 5 + 4 - 4 = 5$

5. $19 - 3 = 10 + 6 = 16$

6. $11 - 3 = 7 + 1 = 8$

7. $7 + 9 + 3 = 10 + 9 = 19$

8. $9 + 6 - 7 = 2 + 6 = 8$

9. $8 + 8 - 9 = 7 + 9 - 9 = 7$

10. $16 - 8 + 6 = 14 - 8 + 8 = 14$

11. $18 + 16 = 20 + 14 = 34$

12. $35 - 19 = 35 - 20 + 1 = 16$

13. $56 + 39 = 55 + 40 = 95$

14. $85 - 58 = 85 - 60 + 2 = 27$

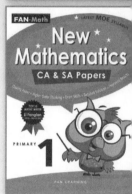